Robert Pattinson

By Robin Johnson

Crabtree Publishing Company
www.crabtreebooks.com

Crabtree Publishing Company
www.crabtreebooks.com

Author: Robin Johnson
Publishing plan research and development:
  Sean Charlebois, Reagan Miller
  Crabtree Publishing Company
Project coordinator: Kathy Middleton
Photo research: Crystal Sikkens
Editors: Molly Aloian, Crystal Sikkens
Proofreader and Indexer: Wendy Scavuzzo
Designer: Ken Wright
**Production coordinator and Prepress
  technician:** Ken Wright

Every effort has been made to trace copyright holders and to obtain their permission for use of copyright material. The authors and publishers would be pleased to rectify any error or omission in future editions. All the Internet addresses given in this book were correct at the time of going to press. The author and publishers regret any inconvenience caused if addresses have changed or sites have ceased to exist, but can accept no responsibility for any such changes.

Photographs:
Associated Press: pages 9, 18
Corbis: © Toby Melville/Reuters: page 13;
  © Jazz Archiv/Skupin/dpa: page 14
Keystone Press: © Entertainment Pictures:
  page 6; © Rena Durham/Zumapress: page 7;
  © Ash Knotek/Snappers/Zumapress:
  page 8; © Krestine Havemann/Zumapress:
  page 10–11; Jackson Lee/Zumapress:
  page 12 (right); © Maverick Films/
  Zumapress: page 17; © ADC: page 19;
  © Casey Christie/Zumapress: page 20;
  © Alex J. Berliner/BEImages: page 21;
  © Kat Woronowicz/Zumapress: page 22;
  © Imprint Entertainment: page 23;
  © Summit Entertainment: pages 24, 25;
  © Ian West/PA Wire/PA Photos: page 26;
  © FAME Pictures: page 27
Photoshot: zumapress: cover
Retna Pictures: page 12 (left); © Gilbert
  Flores/CPA: pages 1, 15
Shutterstock: pages 4, 5, 16, 28

Library and Archives Canada Cataloguing in Publication

Johnson, Robin (Robin R.)
  Robert Pattinson / Robin Johnson.

(Superstars!)
Includes index.
Issued also in an electronic format.
ISBN 978-0-7787-7251-4 (bound).--ISBN 978-0-7787-7260-6 (pbk.)

  1. Pattinson, Robert, 1986- --Juvenile literature. 2. Actors--
Great Britain--Biography--Juvenile literature. I. Title. II. Series:
Superstars! (St. Catharines, Ont.)

PN2598.P36J64 2011   j791.4302'8092   C2010-904686-2

Library of Congress Cataloging-in-Publication Data

Johnson, Robin (Robin R.)
  Robert Pattinson / by Robin Johnson.
    p. cm. -- (Superstars!)
  Includes index.
  ISBN 978-0-7787-7260-6 (pbk. : alk. paper) --
  ISBN 978-0-7787-7251-4 (reinforced library binding : alk. paper) --
  ISBN 978-1-4271-9556-2 (electronic (pdf))
  1. Pattinson, Robert, 1986---Juvenile literature. 2. Motion picture
actors and actresses Juvenile literature.--Great Britain--Biography
I. Title. II. Series.

PN2598.P36J64 2010
792.02'8092--dc22
[B]
                                                        2010027905

Crabtree Publishing Company

www.crabtreebooks.com   1-800-387-7650

Printed in the USA/102010/SP20100915

Published in Canada
Crabtree Publishing
616 Welland Ave.
St. Catharines, ON
L2M 5V6

Published in the United States
Crabtree Publishing
PMB 59051
350 Fifth Avenue, 59th Floor
New York, New York 10118

Published in the United Kingdom
Crabtree Publishing
Maritime House
Basin Road North, Hove
BN41 1WR

Published in Australia
Crabtree Publishing
386 Mt. Alexander Rd.
Ascot Vale (Melbourne)
VIC 3032

CONTENTS

Words that are defined in the glossary are in **bold** type the first time they appear in the text.

Tall, Dark, and Vampire

Twilight is usually defined as "the time of day after sunset." For millions of young people, however, it is defined as Robert Pattinson and the hit vampire movies in which he stars. The romantic fantasy films have rocketed the British actor to fame. However, Robert is more than just a bloodthirsty heartthrob with great hair.

EARLY INFLUENCE

Robert Pattinson was inspired by Jack Nicholson. After watching the movie *One Flew Over the Cuckoo's Nest* when he was 13, he started to dress like him and copy his accent and mannerisms. He believes some of that stayed with him.

Meet Robert

Robert Pattinson has starred in several plays and films. He had a leading role in three of the most popular movies to ever hit the big screen. He has won awards for his acting, his on-screen fighting, and even his kissing! He is also a talented musician who performs on some of his films' **soundtracks**.

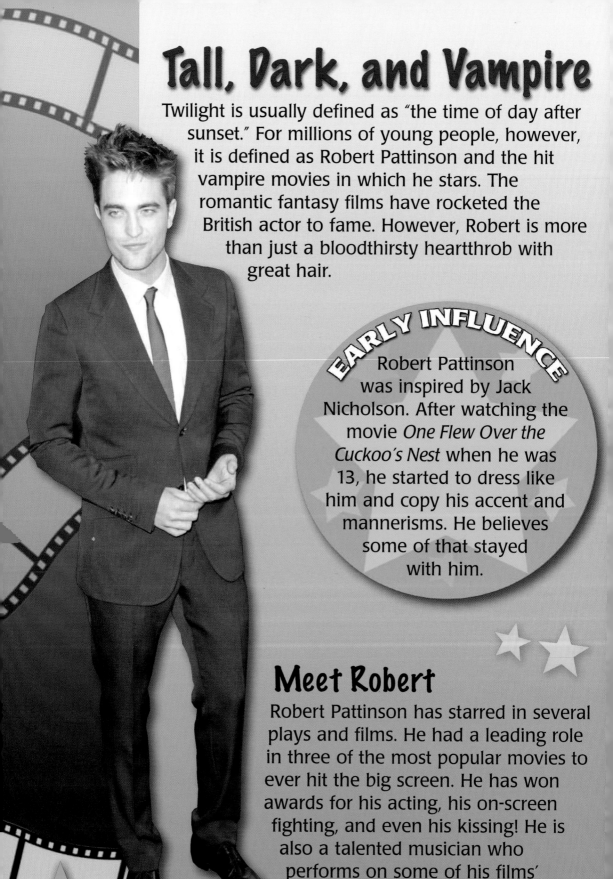

4

Drop-Dead Gorgeous

Robert Pattinson is also famous for being so handsome. He is known for his bushy eyebrows and his brooding stare. His most famous feature, however, is his hair. Robert's thick, **tousled** brown hair has captured the attention of adoring girls—and jealous boys—around the world.

Dreamy Vampire

Robert became famous for playing a dreamy vampire named Edward Cullen in the movie *Twilight* in 2008. Vampires are fictional creatures that appear in many fantasy films and books. They are **undead**—deceased people who act as though they are alive. Vampires are said to rise at night to drink the blood of humans and other living things.

Robert captured the attention of **mortals** again when he starred in *Twilight*'s hit **sequels**, *The Twilight Saga: New Moon* in 2009 and *The Twilight Saga: Eclipse* in 2010. The vampire romance films were wildly popular with preteens and teens everywhere.

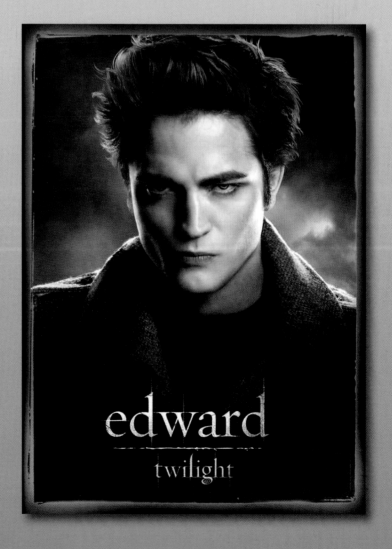

edward
twilight

Name Game

Robert Pattinson's name is known around the world. It seems the teen idol does not love his famous name as much as his fans do, though. In an interview on MTV, Robert invented the names "Spunk Ransom" and "Ransom Spunk." He jokingly asked people to call him one of those names instead. Now, fans sometimes do! When he was a child, Robert's nickname was "Patty." Today, fans usually just call him "Rob" or "RPattz."

Style File

While millions of girls study every aspect of Robert's appearance, the actor himself does not. He prefers a casual, messy style that he describes as "looking terrible." In an interview in *Vanity Fair* magazine, Robert admitted, "Truly, I wear the same thing every day. I don't know how to use a washer machine."

Rising Star

Before he rose from the grave in *Twilight*, Robert rose to fame in a Harry Potter movie. He also appeared in several plays and other films, showing a talent for acting at an early age.

A Star Is Born

Robert Thomas Pattinson was born on May 13, 1986, in London, England. He grew up in Barnes, a wealthy **suburb** of London. He lived with his parents and two older sisters Elizabeth and Victoria. His mother Clare worked as a scout for a modeling agency. His father Richard imported and sold classic cars.

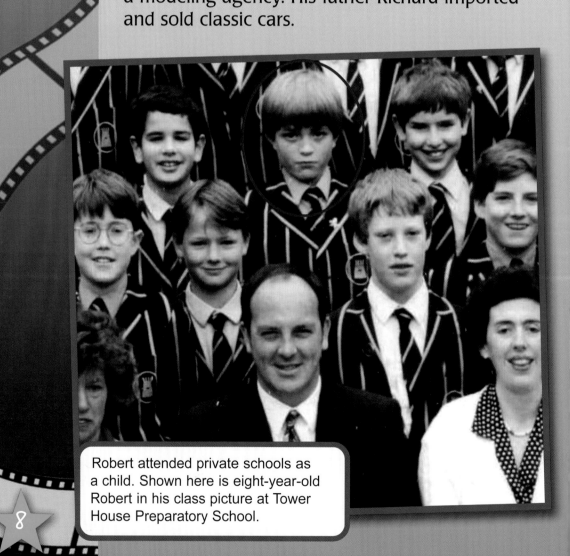

Robert attended private schools as a child. Shown here is eight-year-old Robert in his class picture at Tower House Preparatory School.

Sister Act

Robert's sister Elizabeth—who is called Lizzy—is a popular singer and songwriter. She was "discovered" at the age of 17! Since then, she has toured with the band Aurora and has had three Top 20 dance hits in England. She also performs background vocals on the *Twilight* soundtrack.

Robert's sister Lizzy Pattinson performed at the Wireless Music Festival in Hyde Park, London.

First Act

At school, he was more interested in theater than his lessons. He began acting in school plays when he was just six years old. He starred in *Lord of the Flies* and other productions. He later joined a number of local theater companies. There, he performed in **amateur** plays and musicals, including *Our Town*, *Anything Goes*, and *Macbeth*.

Robert played the role of "Robert" in the Tower House Preparatory School's production of *Lord of the Flies*.

Music Man

Robert began playing the piano when he was three or four years old. He picked up classical guitar at the age of five. He is a talented musician, singer, and songwriter. In an interview in *Vanity Fair* magazine, he said, "I play a lot of music. That's what I wanted to do before the acting thing accidentally took off."

He Said It

SISTERLY LOVE

Up until Robert was 12 years old his sisters would dress him up as a girl! They told people his name was "Claudia." Perhaps that was the start of Robert's acting career!

A Model Student

When he was 12 years old, Robert began working as a model. His tall frame—he is now more than six feet (1.8 m) tall—and good looks made him a natural choice for the job. He worked as a model for four years. Although he did some fashion shows and photo shoots, Robert claims he had "the most unsuccessful modeling career."

In 2004, at the age of 17, Robert landed his first **professional** acting job. He had a small part in a made-for-television fantasy film called *Ring of the Nibelungs*. The film was called *Dark Kingdom: The Dragon King* when it was shown on TV in the United States. Robert also landed a supporting role that year in the feature film *Vanity Fair*. Although his part was cut from the final version of the film that was released in theaters, Robert's performance can be seen in the DVD version.

Magic Moment

Robert's big break came when he was cast in the fourth Harry Potter film. He was cast as Cedric Diggory in *Harry Potter and the Goblet of Fire*. Like previous Harry Potter films, *Goblet of Fire* was a huge success. It made more than $895 million during the 20 weeks it played in theaters—more than any other film in 2005. Both viewers and critics loved the movie. Robert became popular with **muggles** (and wizards) around the world.

Robert Pattinson arrives at the U.S. premiere for *Harry Potter and the Goblet of Fire.*

Meet Cedric

Cedric Diggory is a handsome young wizard in *Harry Potter and the Goblet of Fire.* He is a model student at Hogwarts School of Witchcraft and Wizardry. He lives in the school's Hufflepuff House and is the captain of its **Quidditch** team. In *Goblet of Fire,* Cedric competes against Harry Potter—played in the movie by British actor Daniel Radcliffe—in a magic competition. He also competes with him for the heart of a pretty young witch named Cho Chang (played by Scottish actress Katie Leung). Cedric proves in the film that, sadly, all is not fair in love and magic.

British actors in *Goblet of Fire* from left to right: Stanislav Ianevski, Clé mence Poé sy, Rupert Grint, Emma Watson, Daniel Radcliffe, Katie Leung, and Robert Pattinson

He Said It

*"The day before [the Goblet of Fire **premiere**] I was just sitting in Leicester Square, happily being ignored by everyone. Then suddenly strangers are screaming your name. Amazing!"*
—In an interview in the *Telegraph*, 2005

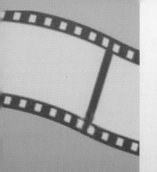

Made for TV

In 2006, Robert turned from a magical wizard into a World War II pilot. He starred in the British television film *The Haunted Airman*. In the film, he plays the part of Toby Jugg, a pilot who is shot down and paralyzed during World War II. The following year, Robert had a supporting role in the made-for-TV British movie *The Bad Mother's Handbook*. He plays a sweet, shy guy who cares for his pregnant, broken-hearted friend.

Robert poses in front of a poster featuring his character Cedric Diggory in *Harry Potter and the Goblet of Fire*.

The Magic Continues

In 2007, Robert brought Cedric Diggory back to life in the feature film *Harry Potter and the Order of the Phoenix*. The fifth Harry Potter movie continued the adventures of Harry and his wizard friends. Although Cedric appears only in flashbacks in *Order of the Phoenix*, the film's huge success helped Robert continue his magical rise to fame.

The Language of Love

Robert spoke in his native British accent in Harry Potter and his other early films. It was not until his role in *Twilight* that he had to use an American accent. Robert learned the accent by watching American movies when he was growing up in England.

Shy Guy

Robert Pattinson is a reluctant superstar. He is shy and uncomfortable in the spotlight. Crowds make him nervous—and when he feels nervous, he blushes, laughs, or babbles. Robert would rather stay home and play his guitar than go out and party. Like many fans of the Harry Potter and Twilight series, he also likes to read books and watch movies.

The Twilight Years

Robert Pattinson was magical in the Harry Potter films. It was his role as Edward Cullen in *Twilight*, however, that made him truly **immortal**.

HUNGRY READERS

Since the release of the book *Twilight* in October 2005, the series has sold over 100 million copies worldwide, with translations in 38 different languages.

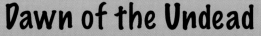

Twilight's leading actors: Robert Pattinson, Kristen Stewart, and Taylor Lautner

Dawn of the Undead

In 2008, Christmas came early for many girls. The feature film *Twilight* opened in theaters on November 21. The movie made nearly $36 million that day! Its leading actors became instant superstars.

The movie *Twilight* is based on the hugely popular novel of the same name. *Twilight* is the first book in a series of vampire romance novels written by Stephenie Meyer. The book has captured the imaginations—and hearts—of people everywhere. It hit bookstores in October 2005 and became an instant bestseller.

Twilight Zone

Twilight is a fantasy romance for preteens and teens. It tells the story of Isabella "Bella" Swan and Edward Cullen. Bella, played by American actress Kristen Stewart, is a sweet 17-year-old girl. She falls in love with Edward, a handsome boy in her biology class. She later discovers Edward is a blood-sucking vampire. Their dangerous and complicated romance forms the basis of the book and movie.

Robert Pattinson and Kristen Stewart share a moment on screen as Edward and Bella in the movie *Twilight*.

She Said It

"He grinned his crooked smile at me, stopping my breath and my heart. I couldn't imagine how an angel could be any more glorious. There was nothing about him that could be improved upon."
—Bella Swan, describing Edward Cullen in the book *Twilight* (2005)

Love at First Bite

Robert and Kristen Stewart are rumored to be a real-life couple. They definitely heat up the screen when they are together. In fact, they have won numerous awards for best movie kiss from MTV and the Teen Choice Awards! Robert was previously linked to Harry Potter co-star Katie Leung, actress Camilla Belle, and *Twilight* co-star Nikki Reed.

He Said It

"[Bella] does not see a single flaw in him at all. It's a very traditional aspect of first or young love. So, it took me ages to think of it, but it ended up being really simple: if you are in love with someone, you can't see any flaw in the other person. So I finally figured out that I didn't have to play the most beautiful man on the planet, but just play a man in love."
—On playing Edward, in *Vanity Fair*, November 2008

Robert plays the role of Edward in the movie *Twilight*. Edward Anthony Masen Cullen is a 108-year-old vampire trapped in the body of a 17-year-old boy. He is described in the *Twilight* book as "devastatingly inhumanly beautiful." He has a "too-perfect face" and a voice "like melting honey." Like Robert, Edward is tall, dark, and handsome. Unlike Robert, Edward must drink blood to survive. He has sworn not to drink human blood, though, and instead seeks out the blood of animals.

Less Than Perfect

More than 5,000 actors auditioned for the role of Edward Cullen! When Robert first read the *Twilight* script, he was reluctant to play the part. He felt he could not live up to the character's perfect image. Unfortunately, many people agreed with him.

Author Stephenie Meyer's first choice for the part was British actor Henry Cavill. Producers feared, however, that the 24-year-old actor would not be convincing as a 17-year-old boy. *Twilight* fans wanted *Star Wars* star Hayden Christensen, British actor Orlando Bloom, or musician Gerard Way to bring their favorite vampire to life. When it was announced that Robert would play the lead vampire in the movie, **devoted** fans of the Twilight books protested. They felt that Robert—who was not very well known at the time—was not attractive or talented enough to play their beloved Edward. An amazing 75,000 people signed an online **petition** against casting him! Others—including Stephenie Meyer—publicly supported him.

Robert as the young vampire Edward Cullen

DRIVER'S SEAT

Robert learned how to drive on the set of *Twilight*. He was given a ten-hour crash course so he could shoot the driving scenes in the movie.

She Said It

"I am ecstatic with [the film studio's] choice for Edward. There are very few actors who can look both dangerous and beautiful at the same time, and even fewer who I can picture in my head as Edward. Robert Pattinson is going to be amazing."
—*Twilight* author Stephenie Meyer, on StephenieMeyer.com, December 2007

Twi-hard with a Vengeance

The most devoted fans of the Twilight series are called Twi-hards. "Twi-hard" is a combination of the words "Twilight" and "die-hard." A die-hard fan is one who has very strong, even stubborn, feelings about someone or something. Most Twi-hards are preteen or teen girls, although many older women are fans, too. Twi-hards are **passionate** about the Twilight stories and characters. They know everything about the books and movies and often quote lines from them. They are also called Twilighters or fanpires.

These Twi-hards have camped out to be among the first people to see the new *Eclipse* movie.

Vampire Diaries

To help prepare for the role of Edward Cullen, Robert began writing a journal—as Edward! He also separated himself from his family and friends. Robert wanted to experience the loneliness and **isolation** that an immortal vampire would feel.

Change of Heart

After seeing Robert's performance in the film—usually more than once—most Twi-hards have changed their minds. Robert is now accepted as the dreamiest vampire to ever live—or not live. Fans scream and cry when Robert is near. They follow him, begging for pictures and autographs. Many even ask Robert to bite their necks!

He Said It

"There's only so much adoration you can take before you start thinking, 'Is a thank you note enough, or do I actually have to say yes [and marry] one of these people?'"
—Discussing *Twilight* fans, in *Rolling Stone*, December 2008

Beyond the Grave

Today, Robert continues to prove he is more than just a hunky heartthrob. He recently starred in a string of films—with neither a wizard nor a vampire in sight. He also returns to theaters as Edward Cullen in the sequels to *Twilight*.

How to Be a Star

In 2009, the British feature film *How to Be* was released in the United States. Robert had the lead role—a troubled young man named Art—in the film. Art moves back home with his parents and hires a doctor to help him become "more normal." Robert's performance in the film earned him the Best Actor award at a **film festival**. It also helped him earn a reputation as a serious actor.

DOIN' FINE!

Robert performed three original songs on the *How to Be* soundtrack. The songs were— "Chokin' on the Dust Part 1," "Chokin' on the Dust Part 2," and "Doin' Fine."

Many *New Moon* moviegoers wore "Team Edward" or "Team Jacob" gear and debated which handsome creature Bella should choose.

Twice Bitten

The fan favorite of 2009, however, was the hit sequel to *Twilight*. Robert returned as dashing vampire Edward Cullen in *The Twilight Saga: New Moon*, which opened in theaters on November 20. Devoted fans bought show tickets weeks in advance and lined up at theaters days before the premiere! *New Moon* set new attendance records, making more than $72 million in the United States and Canada that day and more than $140 million in its first weekend. Although most Twi-hards loved the film's big-budget special effects and larger-than-life love triangle, most critics were not impressed with *New Moon*.

A scene from *New Moon* shows Edward ending his relationship with Bella.

In the film, Edward ends his relationship with Bella to protect her from his bloodthirsty family. He moves away, leaving Bella heartbroken and lonely. She finds comfort and safety with her friend Jacob Black (played by teen idol Taylor Lautner). Bella later discovers that Jacob is a **werewolf** and sworn enemy of the vampires. Bella is reunited with Edward, and the couple learns that mortal Bella must be killed—or be transformed into a vampire forever.

The Saga Continues

The Twilight Saga: Eclipse—the highly anticipated third movie in the Twilight series—opened in theaters on June 30, 2010. The film took in $68.5 million on the opening day. Approximately $30 million was from ticket sales for the midnight and early morning viewings.

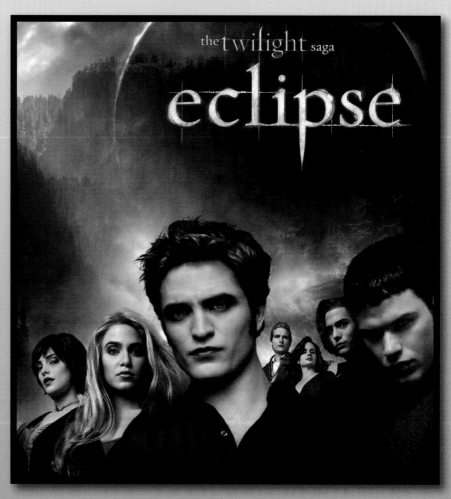

He Said It

"Isabella Swan, I promise to love you every moment of forever. Would you do me the extraordinary honor of marrying me?"

—Edward Cullen, proposing to Bella Swan in the movie *Eclipse*

The film is based on the third book in the Twilight series. In the novel, Edward's family joins forces with Jacob's wolf pack to defeat an army of murderous vampires. Bella realizes that she loves both Edward and Jacob, and she must decide between the two men. In the film, Robert once again brought vampire Edward Cullen to life—continuing to steal hearts around the world.

Jacob and Edward from the movie *Eclipse*

The Twilight finale, *The Twilight Saga: Breaking Dawn,* will begin filming in the fall of 2010. The novel—which spans more than 750 pages—will be divided into two feature films. *The Twilight Saga: Breaking Dawn Part 1* is scheduled to be released on November 18, 2011. *Breaking Dawn Part 2* is planned to open in theaters a year later on November 16, 2012.

Remember Him

Robert also starred in the movie *Remember Me*, which opened in theaters in March 2010. The film is a romantic drama featuring Emilie de Ravin and Pierce Brosnan. Robert plays the part of Tyler Roth, a young man who struggles to keep his romance alive while dealing with the death of his brother. *Remember Me* was a new challenge for its popular young star—and one his fans are sure to remember.

Friends and Captives

In addition to *Breaking Dawn Part 1*, Robert will also appear in three other films all scheduled to hit theaters in 2011. He is starring opposite Uma Thurman in *Bel Ami*. In the film, Robert will be playing a French journalist who charms his way to the top. Robert then moves on to play the part of a veterinarian for a traveling circus and falls in love with the wife (Reese Witherspoon) of an abusive animal trainer in the film *Water for Elephants*. Robert's third film scheduled to be released in 2011 is the western *Unbound Captives*. Robert is playing a boy who is kidnapped and raised by **Comanches**. Robert describes his character—who speaks only Comanche—as someone who "can't really be more different from Edward."

Water for Elephants, set to be released in 2011, stars Robert Pattinson and Reese Witherspoon.

RPattz Forever

Whether Robert Pattinson plays a magical wizard, a conflicted vampire, or someone a little less monstrous, moviegoers continue to fall in love with him and his characters. He is an award-winning actor and a talented musician who will be admired for his work—and his immortal hair—for years to come.

He Said It

"I'm not massively concerned about doing lots of acting jobs. If it all just went, right now, I'd be like, 'All right. I don't really care.'...I think it'd be much worse to do a load of stuff that's really bad...The only thing I want from anything is to not be embarrassed."
—In GQ magazine, April 2009

Timeline

1986: Robert Thomas Pattinson is born in London, England, on May 13.

1992: He begins acting in school plays at the age of six.

1998: The tall, handsome preteen begins working as a model.

2004: He lands a small part in the German television fantasy film *Ring of the Nibelungs*, which is called *Dark Kingdom: The Dragon King* in the United States.

2005: The feature film *Harry Potter and the Goblet of Fire* is released, with Robert playing Cedric Diggory.

2006: Robert plays the lead role in the British television film *The Haunted Airman*.

2007: He appears in *The Bad Mother's Handbook*, a made-for-TV British drama.

2007: He appears in flashbacks as Cedric Diggory in *Harry Potter and the Order of the Phoenix*.

2008: He stars in the 12-minute film *The Summer House*.

2008: The feature film *Twilight* opens in theaters on November 21, with Robert playing vampire Edward Cullen.

2009: Robert plays leading roles in the films *How to Be* and *Little Ashes*, which premiere in the United States in May.

2009: Robert returns as Edward Cullen in *The Twilight Saga: New Moon*, which opens in theaters on November 20.

2010: Robert executively produces and stars in the film *Remember Me*, which is released in March.

2010: Robert captures audiences again in June when the third Twilight movie *Eclipse* opens in theaters.

2010: Robert films the new movies *Bel Ami*, *Water for Elephants*, *Unbound Captives*, and the fourth Twilight movie *Breaking Dawn Part I*, all scheduled to be released in 2011.

Glossary

amateur Describing someone who acts or performs for fun and not for money

auditioned Tried out for a part with a short performance

Comanche A Native American group and the language spoken by its members

devoted Giving time and attention to a certain cause, activity, or person

film festival: An event in which many movies are viewed and judged

immortal Describing a person or creature who lives forever

isolation A feeling of being alone in the world

mortals Describing people or creatures who can die

muggles People in the Harry Potter series who do not have magical powers

passionate Having strong feelings about someone or something

petition A formal written request for change that is usually signed by many people

premiere The first public showing of a movie, show, or musical performance

professional Describing someone who is paid to perform or do a job

Quidditch A fictional sport played by wizards and witches on flying broomsticks in the Harry Potter series

sequels Books or movies that continue the story told in a previous book or movie

soundtracks Albums of the music featured in movies or television shows

suburb An area of houses on the edge of a city

tousled Tangled and somewhat messy

undead People who have died but act as though they are still alive

werewolf A fictional person with the ability to turn into a wolf-like creature

Find Out More

Websites

Pattinson Online
http://www.robert-pattinson.co.uk
The complete online guide to Robert Pattinson

Robert Pattinson Fan
http://robertpattinson.org
A fan site devoted to everything Robert

Robert Pattinson Life
http://robpattinson.blogspot.com
The hottest RPattz blog spot

The Twilight Saga
http://www.thetwilightsaga.com
The official website for Twilight fans

Books

Adams, Isabelle. *Robert Pattinson: Eternally Yours*. New York: HarperCollins, 2008.

Rusher, Josie. *Robert Pattinson: True Love Never Dies*. London: Orion Books, 2008.

Williams, Mel. *Robert Pattinson: Fated for Fame*. New York: Simon Pulse, 2009.

Index

About the Author

Robin Johnson is a freelance writer and editor. The author of several children's books— including *Ice Hockey and Curling, Rodeo, Show Jumping,* and *The Mississippi River: America's Mighty River*—she has worked in the publishing industry for more than a decade. When she isn't working, she divides her time between renovating her home with her husband, taking her two sons to hockey practice, and exploring back roads.

Superstars!

Today's most exciting, creative, and popular young celebrities are profiled in *Superstars!* Enjoy reading about the life story and rise to fame of your favorite star, from their first breakthrough to superstardom.

Robert Pattinson became famous around the world for playing a dreamy vampire in the *Twilight* movies. But he's more than just a bloodthirsty heartthrob with great hair. He has starred on stage and screen, and is a talented musician.

The Jonas Brothers

Kristen Stewart

M.I.A.

Miley Cyrus

Robert Pattinson

Taylor Swift

Vanessa Hudgens

Zac Efron

Guided Reading: Q

U.S.A. $8.95
Canada $9.95

CRABTREE
Publishing Company
www.crabtreebooks.com

ISBN 978-0-7787-7260-6